HOW TO BUY AMAZON RETURN PALLET

Easy Ways to Make Money with
Amazon's Liquidation Pallets

AARON

GEORGE

CHAPTER 1

WHAT ARE AMAZON RETURN PALLETS?

Amazon has a large number of customers that buy a variety of products from the e-commerce giant. However, purchasers occasionally return products because they dislike them or it is not their style (size, color, or design).

Amazon now takes two steps with the returned item. If the product is not damaged, it is repackaged and resold. The second thing they do is put the goods on pallets and store them.

Amazon sometimes puts these pallets on its website and asks

for bids on them. People who are in the business of selling Amazon pallets bid on them and buy the ones they want.

And this is how Amazon runs its business with pallets. If you are good at it, this could be very useful. It can also make you money if you drop ship for an Amazon company.

When people buy these pallets, they can keep the things that are valuable to them and fix up the rest to sell again. This gives them the chance to make a lot of money.

A consumer can buy more things for less money. But purchasers often buy these Amazon pallets without knowing if the items inside are still in good working order. So, buying these pallets may not be a good idea.

CHAPTER 2

WHERE DO AMAZON RETURNS GO?

Only 8.9% of items bought in stores are returned, but 30% of items bought online are returned. This shouldn't be a surprise, since almost 49% of U.S. retailers offer free return shipping. Customers like it because it's easy, but sellers don't like it because it's hard. It is a fair question to ask where all of the Amazon returns go.

Retailers and Amazon sellers may restock them on virtual shelves, but consider the cost of inspection, repackaging, and relisting. In terms of cost and time savings, disposing of these returned goods makes more financial and temporal sense for firms. As the saying goes, the old must leave and the new must arrive.

This is good news for resellers because not all Amazon returns are faulty or damaged. As we've already said, goods can also be returned for reasons like buyer's remorse, no longer needing the item, or expecting something else. So, most of these customer returns will be brand new and in good condition.

Pallets of customer returns from big stores like Amazon are sold to liquidators, who then sell the items online to resellers and small businesses.

With these online stores, it's easy, quick, and cheap to find high-quality brand-name and non-brand-name products.

In real life, warehouse liquidation is nothing new. To make room for new items, stores have always had to get rid of old stock, customer returns, and seasonal items. Over time, liquidation has just moved online. And as technology has improved, buying Amazon returns online is now as easy as using your computer or phone.

CHAPTER 3

WHY BUY RETURN PALLETS FROM AMAZON?

Getting return pallets from Amazon is easy and can be done by anyone. Some people can start with a line of credit or savings of several hundred to several thousand dollars. When it comes to reselling, there are a lot of options. There are lots of places to buy and sell used things, from flea markets to online marketplaces like Poshmark, ThredUp, OfferUp, and others that are growing quickly.

If you need to stock up on merchandise for your new

business or side hustle, look for these liquidation pallets. If it's sold on the primary market, it's probably accessible on the secondary market. Every day, people all over the world sell items like apparel, electronics, gardening tools, and supplies for health and beauty. Before diving into a particular niche, you can test the waters with a wide range of products to determine what your customers respond to best.

You can also purchase in bulk to receive a sizable amount of merchandise all at once. A company with established resale networks, such as a discount store, a regular presence at flea markets, or a plan to export, would be an excellent fit for this strategy.

Starting your own resale business on Amazon is an excellent idea because the return industry there is substantial. These lots may benefit your resale endeavor given the large variety of goods found on Amazon return pallets.

CHAPTER 4

CAN I BUY RETURN PALLETS FROM AMAZON SAFELY?

It is risk-free to buy Amazon return pallets as long as you do so from a distributor that is approved by Amazon, such as Amazon Liquidation Auctions or Bulq. You may or may not receive items in good quality and condition when you receive an Amazon return pallet.

While some items might be brand-new and still in their original packaging, others might be broken or lacking parts.

Return pallet purchases from Amazon are always a risk. You can make a large sum of money if you take the time to examine and recondition the returned goods.

CHAPTER 5

WHAT KINDS OF PRODUCTS DO THE PALLETS CONTAIN?

Anything might happen.

Sites that sell return pallets, on the other hand, usually have different sections for lot size, brand, merchant, and location.

Depending on where you buy them, they could be bigger things like refrigerators and washing machines, or they could be smaller things like toasters and kettles. There are other stores that sell dresses, accessories, and makeup.

The auction description doesn't say what's inside these brown boxes, which makes them fun and interesting.

CHAPTER 6

WHERE CAN I BUY AN AMAZON RETURN PALLET?

1. Be familiar with how to start selling Amazon return pallets

You must have an Amazon account to purchase Amazon return pallets. Join one of the websites for liquidations that are mentioned later in this book. Any item on the list offered by these liquidation companies may be purchased.

A resale certificate must also be completed by the person buying the pallets in addition to the registration form. You can place a bid on the available pallets in the list after creating an account.

Keep in mind that the resale certificate must be provided together with the account details. If you don't have this, it's advised that you get the necessary information and take appropriate action.

You may not need a certificate to resell in some states or countries. This is a result of some localities not collecting taxes. As a result, if you are from one of these nations, you are secure.

2. Figure out what's needed to start the business.

Selling things from Amazon pallets is easy, and that's the point. But it's very important to know how these things are priced and what makes them less expensive than they used to be.

There are many ways to buy these important Amazon items. For example, you can buy them by pallet or by the truckload.

Remember that these things are sold at a price that has already been set. The second thing to remember is that the discount goes up as the order size goes up.

We don't suggest that you buy everything. Larger pallets should qualify for further reductions. Now you have to assess if the stuff in those pallets will make money.

3. Establish your budget for Amazon return pallets.

In this industry, newcomers frequently make mistakes. For instance, they don't factor in the expenses required by this company. However, you'll waste a lot of money if you don't properly care for it.

If you buy a pallet from an auction company, be careful to factor in the shipping costs. Second, note whether any modifications or repackaging of these items are required. If you said "yes," note those charges as well.

4. Look for reliable suppliers to buy Amazon return pallets from.

Contacting an experienced and reliable seller is one of the most important things you must accomplish. Selling Amazon pallets is a risky business, as you can see.

If you don't take the required actions, such as finding a reliable supplier, it could cost you a lot in terms of quality.

You can research the seller and get opinions from other online retailers. They might provide you with more insight into what will happen.

I suggest using the reputable liquidation websites listed in this book. Utilizing these sites reduces your risk of being scammed because they are known for their quality of service. Because there is a chance of fraud, do your homework first.

5. Expect the expected

Some items will be immediately resalable, while others may require repair or can even be sold for components. Even drastically discounted pallets are still an investment for resellers. As a result, you will return your investment by reselling the things at a profit. Make sure you are aware of the condition of the merchandise you are bidding on and that you have enough time to make any necessary repairs.

Some things that are considered salvage can be useful for people who own repair shops or are looking for replacement parts. Check the manifest for any Amazon return pallets you might be interested in to find out exactly what you will get and how much it is estimated to be worth.

6. Research online reviews.

Making a bookmark for review websites like Trustpilot.com is a fantastic idea. Start compiling your data, whether it's on an Excel sheet or several open tabs to evaluate costs and other auction listings. If you are as informed as possible about the item, the company, the quality of the products, and the return policies, you can choose your bids more wisely. The majority of liquidation product sales are always final. The conditions and limitations, however, differ for every store and marketplace.

7. Consider your shipping costs

Shipping costs are the determining factor when buying something, as any successful shop can tell you. If the shipping costs are higher than the pallet's price for the returned products, do not be alarmed. Set aside money for this expense in your budget before making a bid. If you're within driving distance, you should try to take advantage of the fact that certain retailers might let you pick up pallets from distribution warehouses.

Bulk purchases or shipping consolidation, if possible, can

help reduce some of these costs and prevent you from spending hundreds of dollars on multiple smaller shipments.

CHAPTER 7

Earning money online by selling return pallets

If you want to start your own online business, your best bet is probably to buy pallets of returns from a liquidator and sell them. Because Walmart, Target, and Amazon are willing to take a big loss on their liquidated items, the prices resellers pay for returned items are much lower than at other types of wholesale suppliers.

This means that your company will be able to offer potential customers not only a wide range of high-quality goods but also goods at very low prices that will make them want to buy them. Customers are always looking for a good deal, so if you can give them one, they'll be more likely to shop at your online retail store, buy from you again, and tell their friends and family about it.

Also, because you bought the returns at a low wholesale price, your business is more likely to make a good profit because of the prices you'll pay when you buy from a liquidator. This puts you ahead of the competition.

You can make money online if you follow a few simple rules, get your message out there, charge fair prices, and, most importantly, pay the most for the best product. Why not see what a liquidator can do for your company right now? An online liquidation site can give you all the high-quality returns you need for your growing online retail business at prices you won't find anywhere else. You won't regret it.

CHAPTER 8

HOW MUCH MONEY CAN YOU MAKE SELLING AMAZON RETURN PALLETS?

If you carefully fix up every item in an Amazon return pallet, you can make 30 to 50 percent more money on each pallet you buy.

But you have to check out what's on each pallet. To figure out how much you might make, you should look up each item (if you can) on both the eBay and Amazon apps.

Look at how much each item on the pallet cost and how much it might sell for, and then use a weighting factor to account for broken items.

With time and luck, you'll be able to come up with a set of standard operating procedures for buying and judging things for sale.

CHAPTER 9

THE BEST PLACES TO BUY AMAZON RETURN PALLETS

- Amazon Liquidation Auctions is a good place to start.

Use Amazon Liquidation Auctions as a place to start. Amazon used to think that pallets were a great way to help customers.

After that, the company decided to join forces with B-Stock to make Amazon Liquidation Auctions. Customers can now order directly from Amazon.com through the website, which is now known as a B2B market for big items.

The first thing you need to do is sign up for a B-Stock account. Then you'll be able to bid on the pallets. No fees are taken out of the account that was signed up for. At the moment, only people who live in the US can buy from Amazon and bid on B-Stock.

If you live in Europe, you can sign up at Amazon EU Liquidation and then buy the pallets. Amazon thinks this is a good thing and plans to expand to other important markets.

After you buy the pallet, B-Stock will get in touch with you to find out more about your order before sending the pallet to your address.

- **Direct Liquidation**

The best thing about this site is that it works with so many high-end stores, like Amazon. There are stores like Walmart, Target, and eBay on the website.

Another important part of this website is that you can search using your favorite stores. If you only want pallets from Amazon, for instance, you can use the filter to get everything from that store.

One problem with the website is that it doesn't tell you much about the pallets and the products they hold.

Check out this example of an auction on Walmart.com.

Additionally, you need to exercise caution when it comes to the auction images because they might not accurately depict the goods that are being auctioned.

- **BULQ**

BULQ is the best website if you're not a fan of bidding or auctions.

With BULQ, there's no need to post a bid and then wait for it. It's as simple as adding the item to your cart and paying for it at the register.

Another important factor is BULQ's capacity to reveal what is actually contained in the pallet.

This is not available on other websites that offer liquidation.

So if you're concerned that you won't get what you want, The problem with BULQ is that they don't tell you if the products will work or not.

They could be broken or not work.

Here's what a BULQ list for computer hardware looks like

Not only do you get a better idea of what's on the pallet, but you also know exactly what's inside.

- **888Lots**

888 LOTS

The unique thing about this website is that you can buy single items.

There are no auctions, and most of the prices for the lots are set. As a buyer, you can talk to their sales rep about the price of each lot.

Second, Amazon is where 888 Lots buys most of its products. Because of this, they have included a calculator that shows if the product will make money or not.

Also, their manifest is detailed, like BULQ, and it will tell you what kinds of things are on the pallet.

Like BULQ, 888Lots.com sells a variety of pallets, and like BULQ, each lot's contents and suggested MSRP are listed.

They even give you an Amazon profit calculator to help you decide if it's worth it to sell these things on Amazon.

• **Liquidation**

Liquidation is a site that is similar to BULQ. The biggest difference between them is that Liquidation is based on bidding.

This means that you have to make an account on the site before you can bid on the pallet.

Almost nothing about the contents of the pallet is revealed by liquidation. But there is a way to get around this. Look at the pictures that have been sent in to find out what kinds of products are on the pallet. If you have a sharp eye, you will be better off in this situation.

The bids on high-quality pallets may surpass their actual value because so many individuals use liquidations.

It's possible that a pallet you see without any bids will ultimately prove to be a fantastic value. Monitoring the website for updates and taking the necessary action are the objectives.

This is an illustration of an auction for Amazon-returned goods on Liquidation.com.

If you squint your eyes and look very closely, you can figure out what products and brands are in this mystery package.

But Liquidation.com doesn't say much about what's in the pallets that are for sale

CHAPTER 10

IMPROVING YOUR AMAZON PALLET RETURN BUSINESS

You must develop a strategy when you wish to sell the items you took off from the Amazon return pallet. So let's move forward.

1. Arrange and group the items.

When you buy a pallet, you shouldn't expect the things on it to be organized by category or packed together.

Consider the following scenario: you are buying a pallet that has a phone case with a camera lens on it. On the pallet, there will be a mix of covers with different designs and specifications.

On the opposite side, there will be the lenses. It is necessary to sort the covers by color or specification. Then, make the bundle by placing the lens so that it fits the size of the cover.

This is the hardest thing to do and takes the most time. Consequently, you will require patience. Take your time and do these things right so you don't get a complaint about a missing item when you sell the product.

2. Fix the things if you need to.

In the case of electronics, there is a chance that you will find the items broken or damaged (in the case of clothing). It will be easier to sell these items again if you sort them out and send them to be fixed.

In a similar vein, this is one of the costs that people who are new to this industry don't think about.

And finally, get the best pallet you can afford in case you need to fix it. If the thing is very big, the cost of fixing it might be more than the cost of the thing itself.

To keep the items from being taken by customs, you can also

look for logos and make sure they are printed on the back.

3. Include all required accessories.

The products on the pallet are categorized. Nobody knows whether or not the item's accessories are included in the packaging.

Assume you are acquiring a pallet holding power banks. These power banks may not always come with a charging wire.

You should check to see if the charging cord comes with the package. If it doesn't come with one, buy one and put it in the box. Make sure that all of the product's parts are in the box, and if any are missing, add them.

4. Product inspection

One of the most important operations in this industry is product inspection. Examine and inspect the objects after they have been added. This will show the most important information. You can hire an inspection company or undertake the inspection yourself.

5. Put the items back in the box after you've checked them and put the accessories in the box. It's time to put those things back in their boxes. If you have your brand, you can use your own packaging.

If you don't have one, you can use a simple card box. Just make sure that any important information and the box's contents are written clearly on the packaging.

What documentation do I need to start my Amazon return pallet business?

No documentation is needed to purchase Amazon return pallets.

However, to open an account on a liquidation site, you must first obtain a resale certificate, which is a necessary document. It's critical because you'll need it to create the account.

Can I get a return pallet for Amazon directly from Amazon?

Yes, you can get the pallets straight from Amazon. Amazon has joined forces with B-Stock and is now looking for customers who want to buy items that have been returned.

You have to sign up and give the site the information it needs to bid and buy on B-Stock.

What are the contents of Amazon return pallets?

There are numerous goods available on Amazon pallets. The four categories are clothing, high retail, small (sunglasses, bags, small devices), and large (TV, speakers, furniture)

You can conduct some studies to determine which product is ideal for you.

Conclusion

Purchasing an Amazon return pallet is a terrific way to get items at a lesser price. However, when the cost is cheap, there are more obligations.

For example, you must sort the things, produce a list, add the necessary additions, and repack them.

Selling a return pallet is a time-consuming business, but if done correctly, you may make a lot of money.

Made in United States
Orlando, FL
10 May 2024

46732437R00036